ALL SEGOVIA

Text by María Jesús Herrero Sanz

Editorial Escudo de Oro, S.A.

Historic engraving of the city featuring one of its main symbols, the Roman aqueduct.

HISTORY AND URBAN DEVELOPMENT OF SEGOVIA.

According to legend, Segovia was founded by Hercules Egipcio, a great-grandson of Noah, around the year 1076 BC. What is certain, however, is that the city was settled successively by Iberians, Arevacos, Vacceos and Celts, though it was not until the arrival of the Roman armies, overcoming the furious resistance put up from the Celtic stronghold standing there, that the city took its place in history.

The exact site of the original settlement is unknown, though it seems to have stood in the western section of what is now the walled part of the city, at the lower end of the San Marcos district and on the slopes joining these two areas. The stronghold was at the highest point of the settlement, where the Romans later built parapets and the initial sections of what was to be an splendid castle.

Later, during the struggles of the Imperial period and the subsequent Visigoth invasions, the settlers of ancient *Secuvia* abandoned the heights of the city and installed themselves on the banks of the Eresma and Clamores rivers, mainly from what is now Fuencisla to the Alameda. To judge by the number of temples which had been built, the city must already have reached a considerable size. The Romans made Segovia a **free city,** and it was taken over by the Visigoth king Leovigildo.

As time went by, the people dwelling on the banks

of the *Areva* (Eresma) began to fear for their safety, and moved to the peaks and slopes of what is now Segovia, where they built Christian churches and reconstructed the Alcázar fortress. For their further defense, they raised strong walls around this settlement during the period of repopulation under Alfonso VI and Count Raimundo of Borgoña. However, the streets of this walled city were narrow, steep and provided insufficient space, and the people of Segovia were forced to move beyond the safety of the walls. They built new dwellings on the lower slopes, in what are now the districts of San Millán, El Salvador and Santa Eulalia, and above all in the now Parish of Santa Columba. Little respect was shown for the aqueduct, for buildings sprang up under its very arches, there to remain until the beginning of the 20th century.

Two clearly-defined sections of the city thus came into being, the higher and lower districts. In the former, with the consolidation of the Reconquest, fine new Romanesque churches, great palaces, noble houses and the City Council building were constructed. In the latter, the lower classes dwelt, artisans, labourers and farmers. Here the great monasteries and convents were built, and during the Middle Ages clothmaking and weaving became established, taking advantage of the waters of the nearby Eresma and Clamores rivers. The 15th and 16th centuries were a time of prosperity for the city, when great Renaissance palaces were built, along with the new cathedral, the old building having been devastated during the Wars of the Comuneros. However, the clothmaking industry declined in the 17th century, and little new building work was done. Segovia flourished once more during the following century, when in 1764 the Royal Artillery College was created in the Alcázar, under royal patronage. The War of Independence and the occupation of the city by Carlist troops ruined Segovian industry and decimated the livestock of the surrounding farms. Life in the city became precarious and monotonous: nothing was created and much destroyed. At the

Overall view of Segovia, with the Alcázar in the foreground.

command of the city council, eager for more building land, the gates of San Juan and San Martín were demolished, along with the Romanesque churches of San Facundo, Santa Columba, San Román, San Pablo and others in the lower districts, as well as the convents of La Merced and of Los Huertos.

Misfortune continued with fires in the Alcázar and the synagogue. Later, in the early-20th century, this story was to be repeated with the destruction of the magnificent churches of San Agustín and San Francisco and the increasing loss of the almost entirely preserved medieval district. On the other hand, the late-19th century saw the establishment here of various industries: a pottery factory on the banks of the Eresma, and flour, ceramics, paper and resin works, amongst others.

Since the Civil War, the population of Segovia has doubled to 55,000 and whole new districts have been constructed and new industries installed here. The most important industrial development was the creation in 1961 of the El Cerro industrial estate, which was fully occupied by 1974. Two new industrial zones have since been established close to the city: those of Hontoria and of Valverde del Majano.

The city stretches out on either side of the aqueduct.

Partial view of the city, dominated by the cathedral.

AN OVERALL VIEW OF THE CITY AND ITS MONUMENTS

The city of Segovia stands on the heights of a mountain stretching from east to west, at some one thousand metres above sea level. It is surrounded by two rivers, the Eresma to the north and the Clamores to the south, which meet to the west of the city, at the foot of the Alcázar. In the caves of the Eresma Valley, Neolithic and *vaso campaniforme* remains have been found. Of the first period of Roman domination here, bronze coins (with a man's head on one side and an Iberian horseman and the name of the city on the other) along with bulls and wild boar, roughly sculpted in granite.

The great mystery of the Roman period is the aqueduct, one of the most imposing monuments of the whole Roman Empire, standing proudly in a city which is hardly mentioned in ancient history and whose only other possessions from these times are a few crudely sculpted funeral stones.

Under the Visigoths, Segovia was the seat of the bishopric, though the only surviving remains from this period are the necropoles in the environs of the city, in which bronze fibulae and fine brooches have been found. Of the brief Moorish occupation, only a column with a Moorish capital remains. For a long period of time, the heights on which the city stood was deserted, though life continued in the lower districts. In the 12th century, El-Idrisi wrote that Segovia was not a city but a group of villages whose horses were at the service of the lord of Toledo.

Due to its unusual layout, Segovia has been described as a huge ship, with the Alcázar as its prow and the cathedral as the mainmast.

In 1088, Count Raimundo of Borgoña, the son-in-law of King Alfonso VI, repopulated the city, and life returned once more to the abandoned heights of the city, on which were constructed churches, towered palaces and smaller dwellings for the middle classes. To judge by the many monuments dating back to the period, the 13th century was a period in which the city flourished greatly. There are records of some 30 Romanesque churches, of which around 20 are still standing, mostly still used for their original purpose, though others have been adapted to other functions.

The original cathedral, situated on the esplanade of the Alcázar, has the basic structure of a great Romanesque palace, as do the houses of the Cáceres, the Tower of Hercules and many of the more modest dwellings, particularly in the districts of San Esteban and Las Canongías. There are numerous examples of this style in the churches of San Millán, San Esteban, San Martín, San Juan de los Caballeros and La Trinidad.

The singular aspect of Romanesque in Segovia resides in the use of arched porticoes, supported by paired columns and covering one, two or three sides of the churches. The ornamental richness of the cornices and capitals compensates for the poor structure of the masonry, often covered with wood. The inclusion of these porticoes in the design is explained perhaps by the activities of the guilds and the large number of *cofradías* (brotherhoods), who preferred these covered, sunny spaces for their meetings rather than use the cold interiors of the churches. During the 14th and 15th centuries, the city of Segovia was composed of different ethnic groups, with Christians, Moors and Jews living in perfect harmony. The Christian population was divided amongst three districts, clerics dwelling between the cathedral and the Alcázar, the gentry in the centre and in the eastern section of the city, and the merchants and skilled workers close to the southern city walls. The Jews lived within the walls behind the cathedral, around the Gate of San Andrés, whilst the Moorish population dwelt in the district of San Millán.

Practically the entire Muslim community worked in the building trade and were splendid stonemasons and carpenters. To these workmen we owe the Mudéjar elements in some churches, such as that of San Lorenzo, the monasteries of El Parral and San Antonio el Real, the Alcázar and many houses and palaces. The most outstanding of these Mudéjar motifs is the decorative use of **sgraffito,** involving the use of a stencil to scratch the smooth surface of the plastered wall to obtain a double relief effect, with a smooth, lighter colour against a rough, darker lower surface. Most of the fortified houses and palaces of the noble families of Segovia date back to the 15th century: those of the marquises of Moya, de la Hoz, Aguilar, Lozoya, etc. Many of these towered houses are crowned by galleries formerly used to dry wool and which indicate that the wealth of their owners was based either on their flocks of livestock or on the wool trade.

John II and Henry IV of Spain were great lovers of Segovia, converting the Alcázar into a magnificent residence. Henry IV built a great house in the San Martín district his Royal Palace and also resided in the present-day Monastery of San Antonio el Real.

Later, the city took part in the revolt of the Comuneros, defenders of civil liberty against absolute rule on the part of the monarch, a movement in which Juan Bravo played an important role. The crushing of this uprising had no effect on the growing prosperity of the merchants and manufacturers of Segovia, part of whose wealth helped to fund the pious charitable works of the great Spanish mystics, Saint Teresa of Jesus, Saint Francis of Borja and Saint John of the Cross. However, the single great work which united the efforts of the entire populace was the construction of the new cathedral.

After the completion of the cathedral, the population, perhaps exhausted by this enormous feat, carried out no more great enterprises, except for the building of the *Reales Sitios* for the new dynasty. The optimism of the generation of Charles III produced a brilliant but short-lasting flourish of factory building in the city, whilst at the same time, the Segovian Economic Society of Friends of the Country, founded in 1780, concentrated its efforts on stimulating the rebirth of the local economy and cultural advance. The cloth factory of Ortiz de Pan, now the home of the Artillery Regiment, and the School of Arts and Trades (1780) were the bridgeheads of the industrial and cultural resurgence of the city.

Nothing worthy of mention was constructed here during the 19th century, and in general the work of the building industry was limited to the rehabilitation and restyling of the Alcázar, damaged by fire in 1862. Alfonso XII ordered its restoration, commissioning the architects Bermejo and Odriozola to carry it out. The Plaza Mayor was completed in the early 20th century, with a Neo-Plateresque building by Cabello. The most notable buildings of the 1940s were the houses of the Sousa family, now destroyed, that of Nicomedes García and the Civil Government buildings in Plaza del Seminario, along with the Palace of Justice in Calle San Agustín and the sumptuous Caja de Ahorros building in Avenida de Fernández Ladreda. Also interesting is the estate of General Valera in Paseo Nueva and, more recently, the works of Aracil and Curro Inza, the architects of the sausage meat factory "El Acueducto".

Aerial view of Segovia. The aqueduct, the heraldic emblem of the city, is one of the world's most important examples of Roman engineering.

View of the aqueduct at dawn.

OUTSTANDING MONUMENTS

THE AQUEDUCT

The aqueduct is the symbol of Segovia and the most important Roman remains in Spain. This is one of the most interesting of all monuments of the ancient world and is the most splendid synthesis of art and technique achieved by the Roman civilisation. Like all great undertakings, its origins have become legendary: Diego de Colmenares attributed its construction to Hercules, whilst some have even named the Devil as its architect.

According to legend, there once lived in the city a young water-seller by the name of Juanilla, who came down to the city every day to fetch water. This work became harder and harder for her as the days went by, until finally she declared ''I would sell my soul to the Devil if he would make the water reach my house'', and Satan agreed to the bargain. The young girl argued that he could only have her soul if the water reached her house before the cock crowed, then, realising the terrible sin she had committed, she ran home and locked herself in to pray for forgiveness. That night, strange noises were heard, and Juanilla trembled with fear. She carried on praying, and the cock crowed when just one more stone was needed to complete the work of the Devil. Her prayers had saved her at the last minute, for they had brought day-break earlier than usual. The people of Azoguejo laid the last stone of this beautiful

In Plaza del Azoguejo, the aqueduct reaches its greatest height, 28.90 metres.

Puente Seca (Dry Bridge), as it was formerly known. What is true is that the exact date of the construction of the Aqueduct is unknown, for whilst traditional theories indicate that it was built under the Emperor Trajan, more recent studies have suggested that it was actually undertaken under the reign of Nerva. However this may be, the aqueduct was certainly built during the second half of the 1st century AD or the early years of the 2nd. The structure was dry-built from blocks of ashlar, dressed so as to require no kind of mortar. To hoist these blocks up, hooks were used. The weight of the stone forced the hooks to close into pre-prepared slots which are still visible in the blocks today. The use of ropes, poles and wooden scaffolding made the work possible. In 1974 the aqueduct celebrated two thousand years of existence.

The aqueduct is 728 metres in length, with a maximum height of 28.90 metres, reached in El Azoguejo. One section, from the San Ildefonso road to Plaza Día Sanz, consists of 75 single arches which gradually get wider. There is a second stretch which is double-storeyed to take it over the steepest part of the hill, and this consists of 88 arches. There are four more single arches within the walled part of the city, making a total of 167.

This singular monument has undergone many transformations and restorations, one of the most extensive taking place under the Catholic Monarchs, who replaced the original semicircular arches found

in the first section by 36 Gothic arches. This reconstruction was carried out by a Hieronymite monk from El Parral, Juan de Escobedo, who thus repaired the destruction wrought on the aqueduct by Al-Mamun, Moorish king of Toledo, in 1072.

The plaque* in the Azoguejo, under the niches, formerly bore an inscription in bronze referring to the foundation of the aqueduct. In 1520, stone statues of the Virgin Mary and Saint Sebastian were placed in these niches.

Water flowed along the channel at the top of the aqueduct right up until 1884. The water came from the River Acedbeda in the Sierra de Riofrío, some 15 kilometres from Segovia. On arrival in the city, the water came to the first water tower, Almenara, where excess water was evacuated, allowing just 20 litres per second to pass. After another 780 metres, it came to the second water tower with its large cistern used to decant suspended sand and to eliminate floating matter. The water then ran freely once more to the stones which had been miraculously transformed into a huge winged arch, converting its flow into pure art.

THE WALLS AND CITY GATES

The walls enclosing the hilltop defended by the Eresma and Clamores valleys were constructed during the repopulation under Alfonso VI at the end of the 11th century. This king commissioned his son-in-law, Raimundo of Borgoña to construct the walls encirculing Avila, and it is to be supposed that, as Raimundo is known to have stayed for a time in Segovia, the same thing occurred in the case of this city. The walls begin and end at the Alcázar, and have a length of some three kilometres, though at some points the houses built along them almost hide the original structure.

The aqueduct infuses all who gaze upon it with a sense of majesty and splendour.

There were originally seven gates in these walls, with seven wickets, though four of these gates were demolished in the 19th century, and only three remain; two have been walled up but it is still possible to pass through one of them. Those demolished were the gates of El Sol, La Luna, San Martín and San Juan, leaving those of San Cebrián, Santiago and San Andrés still standing. The first of these, the most simple and interesting, opens over the Eresma Valley, and corresponds to the oldest section of the walls. Beside the Gate of San Cebrián is a stone cross, made at the end of the 16th century.

The Gate of Santiago, which also opens over the Eresma Valley, is a Mudéjar construction, with horseshoe arches. To the east, a well-preserved section of the walls reaches to a point near to the Alcázar. The walls on the other side of the gate were demolished in a landslide during the 1960s.

The Gate of San Andrés, giving access to the old Jewish quarter, opens over the Clamores and was restored under Charles I, with the addition of Mudéjar elements. A stone plaque commerorating the activites of ''Pablo '' a petty thief who lived in the neighbourhood can be seen inside the gate whilst at the top there is a chapel dedicated to the *Virgen del Socorro*.

Puerta de San Andrés.

The cathedral seen from La Piedad.

Aerial view of the cathedral.

RELIGIOUS BUILDINGS

THE CATHEDRAL (Plaza de la Catedral)

The construction of the original Cathedral of Santa María began shortly after the repopulation of Segovia during the reign of Alfonso VII, between 1136 and 1144. This stood in front of the Alcázar and, by the late-15th century, was a conglomerate of buildings from different periods and varying styles. In 1520, the uprising of the Comuneros broke out. The rebels occupied the cathedral and the royalists took over the Alcázar. The resulting battle produced the destruction of the cathedral. The chapter moved first to the Church of San Andrés and later, after a vote, to the Convent of Santa Clara, in the Plaza Mayor.

From the plans submitted for the construction of the new cathedral, the chapter selected that of Juan Gil de Hontañón, then working on the new cathedral in Salamanca. On 8 June 1525, the first stone was laid, after a mass presided over by Bishop Diego de Rivera and a solemn procession.

On the death of Juan Gil in 1526, his assistant García de Cubillos took over the work, until Juan's son, Rodrigo Gil de Hontañón, was made chief architect in September of the same year.

On 15 August 1558, the cathedral had been completed up to the transept, and it was inaugurated with huge festivities. The huge tower, with its Gothic spire, built of mahogany brought from America and gold-covered lead, stood out in the sky. During the

View of the
rear of the
cathedral.

Plaza Mayor and the cathedral.

construction of the new cathedral, the 15th-century Gothic cloister and the stalls from the choir of the old building, the only works that could be salvaged from the destruction caused during the uprisings of the Comuneros, were transferred there. Work on the main chapel began in 1563, the same year as the construction of El Escorial started. After deliberations over its from, a polygonal shape was opted for, providing a fine conclusion to a beautiful, harmonious work.

Work was not finally completed until many years later. In 1614, lightning destroyed the great spire, also starting a fire in the rook, and five years later Juan de Mugaguren restored the tower, giving it its present configuration, twelve metres shorter than the original. At around the same time, Pedro de Brizuela designed the Door of San Frutos, and a few years later the Baroque Chapel of the Sagrario was added. The cathedral was consecrated in 1768, and is 105 metres in length, 50 metres wide and the central nave reaches a height of 33 metres. The tower is 88 metres high. Due to its elegance, slender lines and splendid light, the cathedral is rightly known as the **Lady of the Spanish Cathedrals**.

Crossing the Door of San Frutos, the first chapel on the right is that of La Piedad, containing an impressive altarpiece of the same name, sculpted in 1571 by Juan de Juni. Opposite is a Flemish tryptic of the "Descent from the Cross", an early-16th century piece by Ambrosio Benson. The Gothic screen

Aisle and
the exterior
of the choir,
with statues
of the
Evangelists.

Flemish panel of the ''Virgen de la Pera'', by Ambrosio Benson (16th century).

in the chapel is from the original cathedral. In the third chapel, that of San Cosme and San Damián, the sculptures of ''The Conception'' and of the saints have recently been accredited to Gregorio Fernández. In the last chapel in this section, that of the Concepción, there are fine paintings by the Sevillian painter Ignacio de Ries, a disciple of Zurbarán. This chapel formerly belonged to Pedro de Contreras Miñano, admiral of Philip IV, who used wood brought from the Indias in his own ships for the grilles. This story is illustrated in the wall paintings of the chapel.

In the retrochoir there is a superb marble altar containing the relics of Saint Frutos, by Ventura Rodríguez. This was designed for the chapel of the Palace of Riofrío, though it was never to be placed in its original destination.

The Chapel of Cristo Yacente contains a statue by Gregorio Fernández which is kept in an urn and taken out every year for the Good Friday procession. In the next chapel, that of Sant Bárbara, there is a font donated to the original cathedral by Henry IV, whilst in the adjacent Chapel of Santiago there is a magnificent altarpiece dating back to 1595, by Pedro de Bolduque, as well as paintings by the Segovian artist Alonso de Herrera (around 1600). The Chapel of the Sacramento contains a ''Dying Christ'' by Manuel Pereira, formerly the property of the marquises of Lozoya. The splendid ceramic altar which frames it is by Daniel de Zuloaga (1897).

The main chapel contains a large Neo-Classical altarpiece in marble and bronze, designed by Sabatini. In the centre of this is the 12-century statue of the *Virgen de la Paz*. This was donated to the original cathedral by Henry IV, and was covered in silver in the 18th century.

The stalls in the choir are finely wrought, dating back to the second half of the 15th century, during the bishopry of Juan Arias Dávila. The Plateresque lectern in the centre is by Vasco de la Zarza, and the screens in the choir and main chapel are masterpieces of Baroque grille-work, forged in Elgoibar by the Elorzas in 1733. Special mention must also be made of the splendid stained glass windows in the cathedral, some of them in early Flemish style and others dating back to the 17th century, and of the 18th-century organs.

The organs and the grille of the choir. In the background, the high altar.

Chapterhouse: crucifix (school of Valladolid) and Flemish tapestries of Queen Zenobia.

CATHEDRAL MUSEUM

Though forming part of the cathedral itself, the dependencies devoted to this museum deserve separate mention. The museum is reached through the Chapel of Cristo del Consuelo, whose 15th-century Gothic portal by Juan Guas and Sebastián de Almonacid was taken from the original cathedral and transferred to its present site by Juan Campero. Over the threshold is a late-15th-century flamboyant decoration, with a *Pietà* featuring Saint John and Mary Magdalene. The chapel contains the finely-sculpted tombs of the bishops Raimundo de Losana and Diego de Covarrubias.

Part of the museum is housed in the chapel at the base of the tower, which features paintings attributed to Van Eyck, Berruguete, Morales and other well-known artists, and an interesting collection of reliquaries including one attributed to Benvenuto Cellini. There is also a fine collection of religious gold and silverwork, marble crucifixes and an unusual processional organ dating back to the 18th century. Another important work is the carriage used in the Corpus Cristi processions, the silverwork by Rafael González. In the centre of the chapel is the tomb of Prince Peter, son of Henry II, who was killed when he fell from the arms of his nurse on one of the parapets of the Alcázar. The prince was formerly buried in the original cathedral.

Lectern by Vasco de la Zarza, in the choir.

The chapterhouse is very fine and spacious, its walls decorated by a collection of tapestries woven in Brussels in the 17th century, their illustrations depicting the life of Queen Zenobia. The coffered panels are exquisitely-carved and worked in gold creating a marvellous contrast with the rest of the building. On the rear wall is a 16th-century ''Christ on the Cross'', stretching out his arms in pain, whilst next to this room are paintings, including an impressive work by Valdés Leal.

The museum is completed by another room, situated over the chapterhouse, containing an extraordinary collection of incunabula from the second half of the 15th century, one of the finest collections in Spain, as well as splendid church vestments, reliquaries, documents, including royal decrees, tapstries and a valuable coin collection.

Outside, in the cloister wall, there is the tomb of María del Salto, the Jewess who was flung to her death in La Fuencisla.

16th-century Flemish tapestry in the Mythology Collection.

Custodial carriage in gilded wood and silver, a 17th-century work by Rafael González.

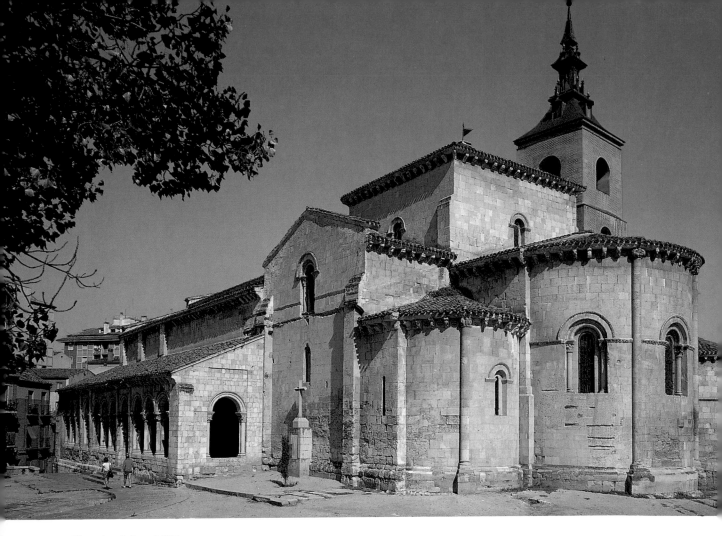

Church of San Millán.

SAN MILLAN (Plaza de San Millán)

This church presides over the district of the same name, formerly occupied by the Moorish population of Segovia. Dating back to the first half of the 12th century, this is one of the oldest churches in the city, and was possibly ordered built by the King of Aragon, Alfonso ''The Battler''. This would explain the extraordinary similarity of San Millán to Jaca Cathedral. The main body of the church consists of a nave and two aisles headed by three apses and a fourth leading to a chapel in the tower. At the north and south, two porticoes with beautiful capitals, the square cupola and the splendid Mozarabic tower complete one of the most magnificent examples of Spanish Romanesque religious architecture.

In the interior, the apse of the nave is outstanding, harmonised by a fine series of arches which were hidden behind a large altarpiece until this was removed, revealing some interesting paintings in the entrance arch to the main chapel. The vault of the cupola has a Moorish structure similar to that of Jaca Cathedral. There are also two fine statues by the Segovian sculptor Aniceto Marinas, and murals by Alonso de Herrera in the baptistry. A recent addition are the magnificent stained glass windows, the work of Muñoz de Pablos.

Various views of the Church of San Millán.

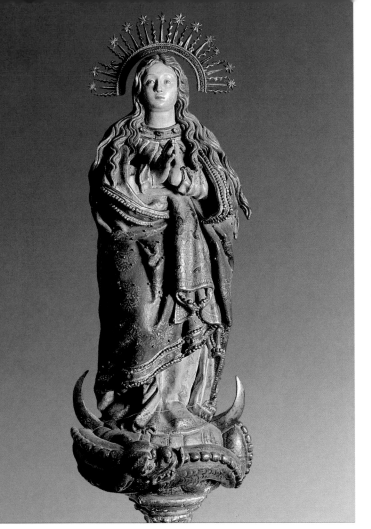

Statue of the Virgen.

LA TRINIDAD
(Calle de la Trinidad, 2)

This is one of the finest and best-conserved churches in Segovia, and was constructed in the 12th century on the site of another, probably Mozarabic church. The interior is of remarkable beauty, particularly the decoration in the form of superimposed arcades in the apse of its only aisle. Beside the lectern is the Gothic Chapel of the Del Campo y Trinidad family, with a splendid portal in the style of Juan Guas. Adjoining the entrance to this is an altarpiece with six panels, commissioned in 1511 by the Del Campo family. Also worthy of admiration is a splendid painting by Ambrosio Benson, representing the "Holy Face", sustained by two angels. This outstanding jewel of architecture, with its fine exterior atrium and portals, combines with the nearby Dominican convent to form a site of remarkable beauty.

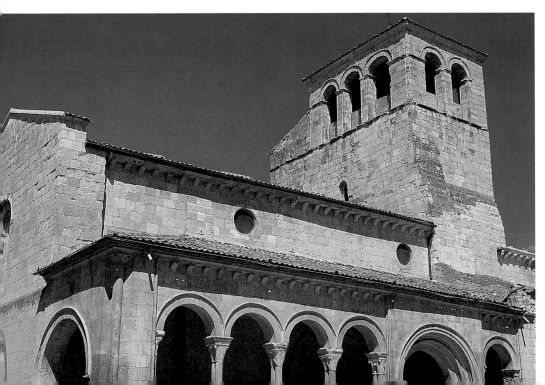

Church of La Trinidad, a 12th-century Romanesque building.

Church of La Trinidad: the presbytery, altarpiece and
"The Holy Face", a painting by Ambrosio Benson.

Church of San Martín: detail of the atrium and Calle Juan Bravo.

SAN MARTIN

(Plaza de las Sirenas)

The Church of San Martín stands in one of the most interesting areas of the city, dominating the slopes of Las Sirenas, and was perhaps the richest and most important parish of the city. Its origins and simple structure correspond to a pre-Romanesque building, with a groundplan in the shape of a Greek cross to which were added the arm of a transept and three apses. The porticoes around three sides of church, with magnificent Romanesque capitals are a later addition. The west front has columns whose statues call to mind the French motifs of Moisac and those of Saint Vincent of Avila. It has two apses, one only recently discovered, as the central apse had disappeared due to one of the numerous extensions made to the building. On the outer wall of the main chapel is an interesting statue of Saint Martin, and the interior contains chapels housing tombs, outstanding of which is that of the Herreras, with a fine altarpiece with 15th-century paintings of the Segovian school. Amongst the valuable statues in the church, worthy of mention are the fine "Saint Francis of Assisi by Pedro de Mena, a moving "Recumbent Christ" by Gregorio Fernández, and a tryptic brought from Flanders at the end of the 16th century by Alonso Moreno, treasurer of the *Real Ingenio de la Casa de la Moneda* (Royal Mint).

Church of San
Martín: detail of the
portico, the main
front and the Herrera
tomb.

Church of La Vera Cruz.

VERA CRUZ

(Carretera de Zamarramala)

The Church of the Vera Cruz, or of the Knights Templar, stands next to the San Marcos district, on the road to Zamarramala. It was constructed by the Knights Templar and consecrated in 1208, according to an inscription in the church. When the Order was dissolved, it passed on to the Knights of Malta, under whose protection it remained until the late-17th century, when it was abandoned. In 1845, it was salvaged by the Provincial Monuments Commission and was declared a national monument in 1919. In 1951, it was returned to the Knights of Malta, who restored it, discovering in the chapel of the tower various late-15th century murals.

The groundplan of Vera Cruz is formed by a twelve-sided polygonal building broken to the east by the triple apse at the head of the church and to the south by the tower. Around the exterior, simple buttresses reinforce the corners of the structure, and there is a cornice of uncut modillions. The interior consists of a small chapel with two floors around which there is an barrel-vaulted ambulatory with twelve sections, separated by arches.

The crossing is covered by a graceful Moorish dome and is higher than the nave. From the upper floor visitors can get a marvellous view of the altar table with its Moorish elements and entwined horseshoe arches supported by small barley-sugar columns. Apprentice knights passed the night in prayer at the foot of this symbolic altar before receiving their coat of arms and entry into knighthood. Archaeologists and other scholars have been attracted to Vera Cruz due to its singular construction, and have compared it with the Temple of Paris, the Church of Christ in Thomar (Portugal) and the Church of Eunate in Navarre. However this may be, the graceful, harmonious, singular structure of this church, founded by the Knights Templar, produces in all visitors a feeling of mystery and enchantment.

Also interesting is the large altarpiece of painted panels on the north side, dating back to 1516 and, in the chapel tower, the Gothic tabernacle which for centuries contained the relic of the *Lignum Crucis*, donated by Pope Honorius III in 1224.

SAN LORENZO
(Plaza de San Lorenzo)

This church stands in the district of the same name, in the Eresma River Valley, surrounded by characteristic buildings forming a square of typical Castilian architecture, its walls adorned with wooden lattice-work. With three magnificent 12th-century Romanesque apses and a superb atrium, this church is an outstanding architectural jewel set off by a brick Romanesque tower, a rarity in Segovia. Inside, in the Plateresque Chapel of San Marcos, there is an altarpiece by the engraver Benito Giralte and the painter Rodrigo de Segovia, commissioned in 1532.

Altarpiece of La Fuencisla, in the Church of La Vera Cruz.

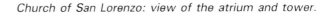

Church of San Lorenzo: view of the atrium and tower.

SAN ESTEBAN (Plaza de San Esteban)

Of the original structure, only the tower and the atrium remain, though these are also the finest elements of the church. The tower consists of five sections supported by a base of the same height as the nave of the church, crowned by a spire, a total of 53 metres high. After the original spire was destroyed by fire in 1896, the tower was rebuilt from above the level of the large traced windows. The restoration process was was completed in 1928. Since 1896, the tower has been a national monument. Inside, there is a 13th-century Stations of the Cross in which Christ is depicted stretching out his right hand, as in the famous ''Cristo de la Vega'' in Toledo. During the most recent restoration work on the church, in the 1960s, the old slate spire was replaced by one of tiles, more in accordance with modern trends in restoration.

Church of San Esteban: the Gothic crucifix.

Church of San Esteban: the presbytery.

Church of El Salvador, which houses the fine triptych entitled "The Adoration of the Magi".

mistakable sign that this was where the image should remain.

Interesting in the nearby Church of El Salvador are its head, tower and, in the main chapel, a fine work of late Castilian Gothic, a sumptuous Chirrigueresque altarpiece.

We should also mention two more Romanesque churches no longer used for worship and whose present functions are different from their original purpose. These are the churches of **San Nicolás,** now the Theatre School, and **San Pedro de los Picos,** restored by its owner as a studio and exhibition room. The first is a 12th-century building within the city walls. During restoration work in the 1960s an interesting 15th-century sepulchre was discovered in

Church of San Nicolás.

one of the apses, containing the preserved remains of a knight and several unusual paintings. Of the second, only the apse and part of the nave remain. It is situated in a pleasant, typical nook of the city, in Paseo de San Juan de la Cruz, close to the Gate of Santiago.

Church of San Juan de los Caballeros, now housing the Zuloaga Museum.

Monastery of El Parral.

MONASTRY OF EL PARRAL

(Alameda del Eresma)

According to legend, this magnificent monastery was founded by Juan Pacheco, Marquis of Villena, who was saved in his hour of need after calling upon the Virgin in this very place. This tale is related on a stone plaque set into the side of the wall that follows the slope leading up to the monastery. In fact, the monastery was founded by Henry IV of Spain, and only the beautiful church can be attributed to the Marquis, whose tomb can be found in the main chapel. In 1477, Juan Guas, his brother Bonifacio and the Segovian Pedro Polido were working on the church, which is built in the style typical of the Hieronymite Order. The Plateresque tower was built by Juan Campero in 1529. Inside the church, there is a splendid gilded polychromatic altarpiece containing carvings (1528) by Juan Rodríguez, Blas Hernández and Jerónimo Pellicer. A statue of the Virgin presides over the nave, the monastery itself being dedicated to Santa María del Parral. On both sides of the altarpiece there are the tombs of Marquis Juan Pacheco and Marquise María de Portocarrero, with statues of them at prayer, crowned by an arch. It is believed that the sculptors were Juan Rodríguez himself and Luis Giraldo, a pupil of Vasco de Zarza, and that the design of the tomb was used as a model by Philip II for the presbytery of the El Escorial monastry. The statues of the twelve apostles in the windows are by Sebastián de Almonacid, and were

begun in 1494. He is also thought to have worked on the unfinished tomb of Beatriz Pacheco, Marquise of Villena and Countess of Medillín, next to the fine sacristy door. The nave and the chapels were used as a mausoleum by many noble families, and the tombs exhibit many different Segovian heraldic symbols.

The dependencies of this vast monastery are built around its various courtyards and are built in a variety of styles. The founder of the monastery, Henry IV, renowned for his protection of the Moors, commissioned builders from the Moorish districts to carry out the work. These masons were so highly skilled in working with brick that they were able to imitate the most delicate stonework using this material. The main cloister, in Gothic Mudéjar style, calls to mind the cloisters of Guadalupe. This Hieronymite convent was abandoned in 1835 when the order was disbanded. The convent became the new seat of the order when it was restablished in 1927. The building has been a National Monument since 1914.

View of the cloister of the Monastery of El Parral.

Monastery of El Parral: the splendid altarpiece over the high altar.

The building was designed by the architect Juan Guas, and has a fine Plateresque portal. The motto of the founders, the Catholic Monarchs, "Tanto Monta", is engraved along the exterior cornice. The church, whose groundplan is typical of the religious architectural style at the time of construction, was stripped of almost all its original adornment during the violent events of the 19th century, which led to its being abandoned. The Provincial *Diputación* converted it into a hostal and, later, into an old people's home.

The Cave of Saint Dominic can still be seen in the grounds of the monastery, with a portal also by Juan Guas. This tiny shrine consists of two chapels, one with rich vaulting and the other an evocative space adorned with Baroque sculptures and tiles from Talavera. On one wall is a wooden sculpture of the Saint, a 16th-century piece attributed to Sebastián de Almonacid.

CONVENT OF SAN ANTONIO EL REAL
(Calle de San Antonio el Real)

King Henry IV, Lord of Segovia from the age of 14, whilst still a prince, commissioned the construction of a palace rich in Gothic and Morisco decorative elements, on a site formerly known as "El Campillo", to the south of the city. Years later, he donated this palace to the Franciscans, who established a monastery there, under the name of San Antonio el Real. In 1488, when the monks moved to the Monastery of San Francisco, now the Artillery Academy, the building was taken over by the nuns of Saint Clare, the present occupants of the buildings.

The church has a simple Gothic portal, and the dome of the main chapel has a magnificent gilded ceiling, in Mudéjar style, of impressive quality and beauty. Also worth seeing is the altarpiece with a Flemish Stations of the Cross, completed in the second half of the 15th century, which is considered by many to be the finest sculpture of the Flemish period to be found in the whole of Europe.

MONASTERY OF SANTA CRUZ LA REAL
(Calle de Cardenal Zúñiga)

At the foot of the city walls, not far from the San Lorenzo district in the Eresma Valley, there are few places in Spain with such an intense spiritual air as the Dominican Convent of Santa Cruz. It was built over the cave chosen to do penance by Saint Dominic Guzmán, who in 1218 founded a monastery of his Order of Preachers here. A few half-buried remains of the original Romanesque apse can still be seen. This splendid monastry was built in 1492 by the Catholic Monarchs, fervent supporters of this Order. Its first prior was Tomás de Torquemada, and on 30 September 1574, Saint Teresa of Jesus went into an ecstatic trance in the chapel leading to the Holy Cave.

Monastery of San Antonio el Real: front and Chamber of the Kings.

Refectory of the Monastery of San Antonio el Real.

Several of the dependencies of the enclosure are open to the public. The sacristy has unusual panelling, and leads to a gallery around a Mudéjar cloister, similar to that of El Parral. This gallery has splendid panelling and contains various statues and paintings, as well as a whitewashed Gothic portal. Three Flemish tryptichs are found in this gallery, framed in Mudéjar plasterwork. These are from the Utrecht school, and date back to the second half of the 15th century. In the centre of each is a sculpture, whilst the sides feature painted panels. The refectory is interesting, containing a fine pulpit from the times of Henry IV. The chapterhouse dates from the same period and has an excellent Mudéjar ceiling. The room which was formerly known as the Chamber of the Kings has excellent panelling and carpets made in Cuenca.

CONVENT OF SANTA ISABEL
(Calle de Santa Isabel)
Not far from the Convent of Antonio el Real is the Convent of Santa Isabel, occupied by Franciscan nuns. It was founded in 1560 by Canon Juan del Hierro. The Gothic chapel contains a fine Plateresque grille, attributed to Cristóbal Andino, and which was taken from the original cathedral. There are also various interesting wooden sculptures, such as the "Virgen de la Leche", a 16th-century piece.

Convent of the Descalced Carmelites.

MONASTERY OF THE DESCALCED CARMELITES
(Alameda de la Fuencisla)

The Monastery of the Descalced Carmelites stands on the same site as a Trinitarian convent, founded in the Eresma Valley in 1206 by Saint John of La Mata. It was founded by Saint John of the Cross in 1586, thanks to the generosity of Ana of Peñalosa. Saint John of the Cross was prior of the monastery from 1588 to 1591. Two years after his death in 1593, his remains were brought from Ubeda to Segovia to be buried in the monastery he had founded, in a sumptuous mausoleum crowned by a high coffer and surrounded by statues of the Carmelite saints.

The monastery grounds, which lie in the site known as "Peñas Grajeras", contain the tiny Chapel of Santa Teresa, and a cyprus tree planted by the saint. A small Carmelite museum in the church contains documents, relics and a painting of "Christ with the Cross" which, according to legend, spoke to Saint John. The church, constructed over the original building in the 17th century, consists of domed cruciform and has a statue of the Virgen of Carmen over a modern altar.

Exterior and interior views of the Arch of Fuencisla.

LA FUENCISLA
(Alameda de la Fuencisla)

Under the craggy heights of the site known as the "Peñas Grajeras" is the Shrine of the Virgen de la Fuencisla, patron saint of Segovia. The original building, constructed in the 13th century, stood on the very site of the Miracle of María del Salto, and the statue of the Virgin was carried from the north door of the cathedral to the shrine, built to commemorate this event. According to legend, a young Jewess, Esther, was to be unjustly flung to her death, but was saved by the Virgin, who heard her cries of "Virgin of the Christians, save me". Esther

Shrine of the Virgen de la Fuencisla.

was converted to Christianity and changed her name to María, becoming popularly known as María del Salto ("of the Jump").

The present shrine was built between 1598 and 1613, designed by Francisco de Mora. The work was carried out by Pedro de Brizuela. It is in the shape of a Latin cross and contains a splendid altarpiece by Pedro de la Torre, with paintings by Francisco Camilo. There is an interesting grille in the presbytery, donated by the Guild of Wool Carders in 1764. The pulpit is a delicate Gothic work, possibly wrought in the foundries of Henry IV, though it was donated as late as 1613.

The Treasure of the Virgen contains valuable mantles and jewellery donated by the people of Segovia over the centuries. Outstanding is the crown, paid for by popular subscription, used in the coronation of the Virgin in 1916.

The Arch of La Fuencisla, in the park, is an 18th-century Baroque work, its unusual bas-reliefs depicting the miracle of the condemned Jewess.

Shrine of La Fuencisla: sacristy.

Shrine of La Fuencisla: presbytery.

Statue of Our Lady of La Fuencisla, patron saint of Segovia.

SAN MIGUEL

(Calle de la Infanta Isabel, 1)

The Romanesque Church of San Miguel formerly stood in the centre of the Plaza Mayor. The atrium provided the setting for the coronation of Isabel the Catholic who was crowned Queen of Castile on 13 December 1474 by decision of the Council of Segovia. The church was destroyed in 1532, and the present building dates back to 1540, constructed further to the south to give more width to the square. The style of this church is similar to that of the cathedral, and was designed by Rodrigo Gil de Hontañón. It contains a magnificent Gothic nave and a splendid altarpiece over the high altar, completed in 1672 by José de Ferreras. The Chapel of Diego de Rueda is interesting, containing fine tombs, as is that in which the famous Segovian doctor Andrés Laguna, who died in 1560, is buried.

The church treasure includes a Gothic chalice with enamel coat of arms and a 16th-century processional cross, the work of the Segovian craftsman Diego Muñoz.

The front of the church features three Romanesque bas-reliefs from the original building, of which that representing Saint Michael is one of the finest Romanesque works to be seen in the city.

Church of San Miguel: high altar.

Church of San Miguel: detail of the main front.

Aerial view of the Alcázar.

PALACES AND HOUSES

THE ALCAZAR

Records referring to the Alcázar by this name go back as far as the 12th century, when it was probably simply a tower surrounded by moated walls. Its exceptional location for the defense of the city, coupled with the growing prosperity of Segovia and the love for the city of the Trastamara ruling family were the main reasons behind its transformation into a noble residence and Oriental-style palace.

There is a beautiful legend which relates that lighting struck the bedroom of Alfonso X, the Wise, sent by God to punish the king who believed himself more intelligent than his Saviour. Dating back to the same period are the remains of proto-Gothic elements and Romanesque windows and capitals, discovered after a fire in 1862 and which form the oldest features of the Alcázar.

The Trastamara family converted the site into a palace after the style of the Thousand and One Nights, employing Moorish plasterers, painters and carpinters. Catalina of Lancaster ordered the decoration of La Galera, whose gilded ceiling imitates the form of a galley. John II commissioned the construction of the magnificent tower which bears his name,

Patio del Reloj.

Parade ground.

and also converted the fortress into a centre of art and culture. Whilst stilll a prince, Henry IV, in his great love for the city, had the Room of Las Pinas decorated in 1452, and a little later he turned his attentions to those of El Solio, the Kings and El Cordón. The turbulent and chaotic times of Henry IV were changed changed by Isabel the Catholic, when on 13 December 1474 the then Princess Isabel and her court left the Alcázar to procede to the Plaza Mayor for her coronation as Queen of Castile.

Charles I was indifferent to the fortress, whilst Philip II carried out wide-reaching alterations and renovations, celebrating his fourth marriage, to Anne of Austria within these walls in 1570. In 1590, Flemish

workers covered the building and its cylindrical towers with steeply sloping slate tiles, fire walls and pointed spires. The result of all this work is the exotic, picturesque sight which meets our eyes as we contemplate this magnificent fortress. Philip II also replaced the Gothic courtyard with the present Herrera-style patio, the work of Diego de Matienzo after the design by Francisco de Mora. Despite the restoration of the Mudéjar roofs the Alcazar took on a more grey and sombre aspect.

Charles III decided to install an Artillery College within these walls, and the opening class was given on 6 May 1764. Thanks to the good cheer of the cadets, the Alcázar recovered for some years the happy at-

The Alcázar overlooks the Eresma River. ▷

54

Tower of Juan II.

Stained glass window in the Alcázar. ▷

mosphere of bygone times, but this was interrupted again on 6 March 1862, when a terrible fire, fanned by strong winds, destroyed practically the whole building. However, hardly had the flames of the fire died out than the people of Segoveia decided that the Alcázar must be rebuilt. The difficult times the country was then going through held up this work until 1940, when Bermejo and Odriozola began on restoration work. Although technically admirable it is a somewhat excessive work, like so many of that time. The drawings made in 1840 by José María Avrial, director of the School of Fine Arts and Trades, provided invaluable assistance for the restoration of the roofing.

A visit to the Alcázar, now converted into the General Military Archives, is most interesting, allowing the imagination to take flight back over history.
The Sala del Solio, or Throne Room, was the first to be restored, adorned on three sides by the original beautiful Moorish frieze, designed by Xadel Alcaide. A 15th-century ceiling was also installed, taken from Urones de Castroponce in Valladolid. Next to be restored was the room of La Galera, uncovering four large windows which revealed the limits of the original building at this point. The plasterwork of the two main walls is original, whilst the arms are on permanent loan form the Lázaro Galdiano Museum in Madrid. One of the minor walls is decorated with a

View of the Sala de las Piñas, the coffering of the Throne Room and the altarpiece in the chapel.

Front of the Palace ⌐
the front of the Pala⌐
the Pala⌐

CASA DE LOS LOZ⌐

(Plaza del Conde de⌐
Opposite the Casa d⌐
built by the Marque⌐
formerly belonged t⌐
charming 12th-cent⌐
beautiful Gothic cou⌐
trance hall. This pal⌐
above the walls, co⌐
sumptuous rooms. T⌐
de San Juan contai⌐
Virgin de Los Remed⌐
statue originally sto⌐
trance gate to the ⌐

CASA DE DIEGO D⌐

(Calle de Escuderos⌐
This house with its⌐
Governor Diego de ⌐
that it belonged to A⌐
is represented on a ⌐
rooms. Although the⌐
the 15th-century Go⌐
galleries and richly d⌐
thy of a visit.

PALACIO DE LOS I⌐

(Plaza del Conde de⌐
This 15th-century ⌐
Heridia family and l⌐
has a highly origin⌐
helmets and a coa⌐
ferocious- looking ⌐
Gothic courtyard, an⌐
ceilings. The buildin⌐
from the Music Con⌐

*Altarpiece
of Santiago,
in the
Alcázar
chapel.*

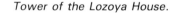
Tower of the Lozoya House.

When the house was inherited by the Marquises de Lozoya in the 17th century they set to restoring and embellishing the original structure. Inside there is a delightful Plateresque courtyard and a charming Renaissance garden. Tiles are used to decorate the chimneys and friezes found in the different rooms. The building once served as residence to the Duke of Wellington during his stay in the city. Many of the works of art that were originally part of the palace, such as the famous Pereira crucifix, can now be found in the *Museo Provincial* and the Cathedral. The Torreon of Lozoya is now used to house the art exhibitions sponsored by the Segovian based Savings Bank *La Caja de Ahorros de Segovia*. The building was acquired quite recently by the bank and is now used as the emblem of its cultural department.

CASA DE LOS PICOS
(Calle de Juan Bravo, 33)
The famous *Casa de los Picos* takes its name from its unusual front with its diamond shaped blocks of stone whose effect of light and shade can be admired by the visitor. It was built in the 15th century by Pedro López de Ayala, Count of Fuensalida and later taken over by the Hoz family at the end of the same century. Their coat of arms can be seen on the keystone of the impressive entrance arch. Tradition has it that the Hoz family ordered the facade to be covered with the diamond shaped stones in order to disassociate it from the name "The Jewish House" by which it was previously known. This type of masonry is frequently found in Italian palaces and it is thought that the architect responsible for the project must have been a member of Juan Guas' circle. Inside the palace there is a fine windowed courtyard with a ceramic panel by Talavera. The splendid city Gate of San Martín originally stood next to the palace but it was knocked down by order of the local authorities in 1883. This building now houses the School of Applied Arts and Crafts.

Front of the L

BISHOP'S P.
(Plaza de Sa
This enormou
with classic
structed in th
the noble Sa
Bishop Muril
palace of the
courtyard ha
tains finely d
trance has a l
is crowned b

House of th

TORREON DE LOZOYA
(Plaza de San Martin)
This 14th-century Gothic tower with its sgraffito designs is the most interesting feature of the *Casa de Lozoya*. Built by the Cuéllar family it was later taken over by the Aguilar family whose coat of arms appears above the central arch of the doorway.

*Original
front of the
House of
Los Picos.*

Tower of Hercules.

Arias Dávila tower.

TORRE DE HERCULES
(Plaza de la Trinidad)

This medieval tower stands inside the walls of the convent of *Santo Domingo el Real*. Built around the year 1200, it contains one of the finest Morisco paintings to be found in Spain. It depicts *fiestas*, tournaments and knightly combat.

At the foot of the staircase there is a granite statue of Hercules with the head of a wild boar which dates back to Roman days. It is from this statue that the tower gets its name. The eastern exterior wall of this huge convent provides us with an idea of how Segovia was during the Roman occupation.

The Church belonging to the Convent was built around the year 1600. Its main chapel contains an alterpiece from the Becerra studio.

TORREON DE ARIAS DAVILA
(Plaza de los Huertos)

The slender tower is the only thing that remains of the 15th century palace built by the Arias Dávila family. It is built in military style with battlements and parapet and the walls are decorated with fine sgraffito designs. To the west of the central battlement is the coat of arms belonging to the Count of Puñonrostro consisting of an eagle, a castle and a cross. The palace was recently restored and now houses the income tax office.

PALACIO DEL MARQUES DEL ARCO

(Calle del Marques del Arco)

In front of the cathederal there stands a fine Renaissance palace built in the second half of the 16th century. Its severe granite front is decorated with railings and balconies of classical style. Beyond the noble entrance hall there lies a delightful Renaissance courtyard with a glazed in gallery above. One of the walls contains some fine sgraffito busts of Roman emperors. This palace, belonging to Cardinal Espinosa who died in 1572, contains some beautiful rooms and valuable works of art.

Fronts of the Palace of the Marquis of El Arco (above) of the House of Deán and of the Palace of the Counts of Cheste.

Front of the
City Hall.

House of the Marquises of Castellanos.

PUBLIC BUILDINGS

THE TOWN HALL
(Plaza Mayor)

Pedro de Brizuela first presented his plans for his Renaissance masterpiece in 1609. However, in 1611 the plans were redrawn to include pillars on the ground floor which were included in the finished building. The completed work has three floors and a simple granite front which contrasted with the brick buildings which surrounded it at the time of construction. The building has two decorative towers from which it was intended to hang the city coat of arms. A project that was never actually put into practice. Inside the building you can see the famous *Sala Blan-* *ca* or White Hall decorated in the style of the Spanish Queen, Isabel II. There is also a valuable tryptich by Benson, a fine alabaster relief and paintings signed by Madrazo.

THE LIBRARY AND HISTORICAL ARCHIVES
(Calle de Juan Bravo)

The Library and Historical Archives are housed in what was once the Royal Prison *Cárcel Real* where the Spanish poet and dramatist, Lope de Vega was held in 1577. The present building dates back to the beginning of the 17th century and shows the influence of Pedro de Brizuela. Granite and rubble were used in its construction, and the top corners are adorned with charming turrets decorated with coats

Doorway to the Church of San Quirce.

of arms, as is the entrance doorway. The windows are protected by strong bars which were formerly checked every night to ensure that nobody had tried to saw through them. The building underwent various reforms during the 18th century and continued to be used as a prison until 1933, when a building in the southern districts of the city began to be used for this purpose. Reforms were carried out in 1946, after which the building has housed the various departments of the Library and Historic Archives. A magnificent Romanesque doorway taken from the Shrine of San Medel, which once stood in the environs of the city, is to be admired in one of the two rooms on the ground floor, now used for art exhibitions and cultural events.

MUNCIPAL ARCHIVES
(Bajada de la Alhóndiga)

The 16th-century construction known as the *Alhóndiga* was originally used as the municipal grain store, until the authorities decided that loans and payments to workers should be made in cash. Such an institution was typical of a city whose economy was based on agriculture. It has a superb Renaissance doorway. The large granite voussoirs around the arch are decorated with balls and shields featuring the city coat of arms. The wooden eaves are decorated with typically Segovian sgraffito designs. The building now houses the Municipal Archives, which contain invaluable documents relating to the history of the city.

THE SAN QUIRCE ACADEMY OF ART HISTORY
(Plaza de San Quirce)

This church with its Romanesque double apse and entrance porch provided the resting place for Diego Enriquez del Castillo, who wrote the chronicals of Henry IV. His Plateresque house can be found a few steps away in the *Calle de la Trinidad*. The church was abandoned during the 19th century but in 1927 it was taken over by the *Universidad Popular Segoviana* and was converted into conference rooms and a library. The main entrance gate and the tower were restored in 1949. The building now houses the San Quirce Academy of Art History which is a dependent body of the *Consejo Superior de Investigaciones Cientificas*

THE ARTILLERY ACADEMY
(Calle de San Francisco)

Not much of the Francisan convent remains after the reforms and improvements that were carried out by the Artillery Academy. The former convent had a large Gothic church where members of the Cáceres family were buried. The beautiful Gothic courtyard can still be seen today. The Franciscan nuns settled here in 1250 and the importance of the convent over the years to come can be seen by its size and its works of art. The Franciscans left the building in

Cloisters of the Artillery Academy.

1862 when the order was secularised. The Artillery Academy which was originally situated in the Alcázar took over the building after the out-break of fire in that area. The church once stood near what is now the main entrance to the Academy and the courtyard can still be seen from here.

DIPUTACION PROVINCIAL
(Calle de San Agustin)

The building which now houses the Diputacíon Provincial was previously the 15th-century palace of the Uceda-Peralta family. This formidable building has a fine granite front and windowed courtyard. It contains valuable works of art and some extremely important documents relating to the history of both the city and the province.

Front of the provincial government building.

PLAZA DEL ALCAZAR

In reality, the name of this square is Plaza de la Reina Victoria Eugenia, but it will always be known as Plaza del Alcázar, as it stands before the walls and towers of this impressive monument at the westernmost point of the city. This beautiful explanade measures 115 metres by 52, and was the site of the original cathedral, destroyed by the Comuneros defending the Alcázar. In the centre of the gardens of the square is a majestic bronze monument to Daoíz y Velarde, by Aniceto Marinas (1910) which was moulded at the national foundry in Trubia. The monument reaches a height of 12.6 metres and is enclosed by a fine grille. The square is bordered by iron railings placed here in 1817 on the occasion of the visit of Ferdinand VII to the city.

Monument to Daoiz y Velarde, in Plaza del Alcázar.

Calle Real.
Calle de los Desamparados.

WALKS AND GARDENS

CALLE REAL

This is Segovia's most famous street, and the name Calle Real is popularly applied to the entire stretch of road from El Azoguejo to Plaza Mayor. Its name responds to the custom of calling the most central and busiest street in all cities ''Calle Real'', and is where the highest concentration of offices, galleries and shops are to be found.

The street, typically of medieval town planning, winds steeply up, and is rather narrow, but is an obligatory part of the itinerary for all festivities and processions held in the city.

Calle Real is divided into three stretches, each with its own name. From El Azoguejo to the *mirador* known as La Canaleja, next to the Casa de los Picos, it bears the name of Calle de Cervantes. This is due to the fact that to celebrate the third centenary of the publication of the first part of Cervante's immortal ''Quijote'', it was agreed that each locality should give the name of the glorious author to one of its streets, and Segovia, though it had already named one óf its streets after Cervantes, decided that the best tribute to him would be to dedicate this stretch of Calle Real to his memory.

The second stretch goes from La Canaleja, on the site where the Gate of San Martín once stood, to Plaza del Corpus, and is known as Calle de Juan Bravo. The road is lined with some of the most im-

Paseo del Salón.

portant buildings in Segovia: Casa de los Picos, Palacio del Conde de Alpuente, Casa de los Tordesillas, the buildings in Plaza de San Martín and the seats of institutions such as the Chamber of Commerce and the Casino de la Unión, an association organising leisure activities. Number 31 of this street contains a quiet little inner courtyard with twisted columns and, in the centre an ailanthus of more than 100 years' antiquity.

Calle Real is completed with the section known as Calle de Isabel la Católica, which goes from Plaza del Corpus to Plaza Mayor. It takes its name from the proclamation of Isabel as Queen of Castile, on 13 December 1474. A dais was raised for this occasion in the atrium of the Church of San Miguel, on its original site in the centre of Plaza Mayor, where there is now a bandstand.

PASEO DEL SALON

This well-known thoroughfare runs along the foot of the city walls, between the now-lost gates Del Sol and De la Luna. Protected from the north wind by the high houses built on the walls, it is a popular meeting-point for the inhabitants of Segovia during the warm winter afternoons or the cool summer evenings. Streets lead down from this promenade to the district of San Andrés and the Arch of San Andrés, joining at the mouth of the Bridge of Sancti Spiritus.

El Salón was formerly known as **El Rastro** due to its proximity to a wicket near the Gate of El Sol, El Rastrillo, the entrance to the city for late-comers after curfew. It was also the site for the slaughter of lambs, and was where the offal from these animals was sold.

Two views of Calle Judería Nueva.

THE JEWISH QUARTERS

During the Middle Ages, Christians and Jews lived side-by-side in peace in Segovia, and persecution, common in other Spanish cities, was unheard of here. In 1412, Queen Catalina of Lancaster issued a decree ordering the Jews to evacuate the area around the Convent of La Merced, between what are now Calle de la Almuzara and Calle del Socorro. The fact that the Catholic Monarchs ordered the two communities to be separated in 1481 is eloquent proof of that the Jews were still in residence throughout the city in those times. This decree was carried out to the letter, and the doors and windows of the houses of Jews adjoining those of Christians were walled up. The Jewish quarters then began to extend along what is now Calle de la Judería Vieja and Calle de La Paz and Calle Orduña.

The old Jewish quarter was centred around the former main synagogue, now the Church of Corpus Cristi. The narrow Calle de la Judería Vieja leads to Calle de Santa Ana, with its well-worn ancient steps. At the end of this road there is a niche with the image of Saint Anna, patron saint of shoe-makers, one of the typical trades of the Jews living in this district. Beyond this point, behind the cathedral, is Plaza del Socorro, with the Gate of San Andrés, the heart of the old Jewish quarter. Here, despite the many alterations carried out, the streets and houses conserve an evocative, moving air of by-gone times. On the other side of Plaza del Socorro is the Calle de la Judería Nueva, a steep, winding street flanked by humble old houses whose windows were walled up. At a bend in this street is a house in which a stone plaque proclaims that here dwelt the Jewish

Calle de San Sebastián.

Plaza del Socorro.

doctor and money-lender Don Mayr, protagonist of the supernatural events of the ''Miracle of the Host'' in 1410. Calle de la Judería Nueva ends in Plaza de la Merced, where the minor synagogue formerly stood.

Calle del Socorro leads to some remains of the walls of the Palace of the Condes del Sol, later the Convent of the Calced Carmelites. In the 18th century, this building was used as the municipal slaughterhouse, now in the industrial zone of the city. Opposite this site, there is a magnificent view of the Alcázar, whilst below runs the Eresma, meeting the Clamores at the foot of the fortress. By the banks of the latter river, on the opposite side, there is a small pine wood on what was formerly the Jewish cemetery, of which tombs still remain.

THE HOUSE OF ANTONIO MACHADO

The poet Antonio Machado came to Segovia towards the end of 1919 to teach French. He stayed here for twelve years, perhaps the most intensely creative period of his career, living in the Calle de los Desamparados, in the middle of the San Esteban district, in a humble dwelling entered through a small courtyard next to a Franciscan convent, the Convent of San Juan de Dios. To this building was later added the Hospital of Desamparados, founded in 1594 by Diego López to care of the poor and abandoned.

In his humble room in this evocative street, Machado wrote such works as "Nuevas Canciones", "Desdichas de la Fortuna", "Don Juan de Mañana", "La Duquesa de Benamejí", and many more, as well as the poem entitled "El Milagro" (The Miracle), which begins as follows:

> *En Segovia, una tarde, de paseo*
> *por la Alameda que el Eresma baña*
> *para leer la Biblia*
> *eché mano al estuche de las gafas*
> *en busca de ese andamio de mis ojos*
> *mi volado balcón de la mirada ....*

The room he occupied has been conserved exactly as it was then, under the care of the Popular University of Segovia, and a bust of this great poet presides over the courtyard of the house.

The house where the poet Antonio Machado lived, and his portrait.

J. UNTURBE
1952

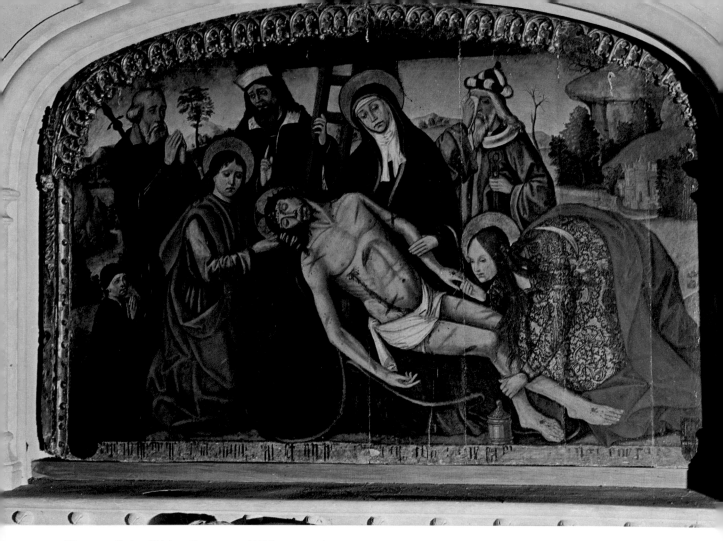

"Descent", by Clérigo Contreras (15th century).

MUSEUMS

PROVINCIAL FINE ARTS MUSEUM
(Calle de San Agustín)

This is housed in a large, rambling 15th-century house known as the Casa del Hidalgo. The building has a fine portal, typical entrance and medieval courtyard. Next to the museum is a Gothic chapel, formerly the Hospital de Viejos, near Plaza de San Martín. The front of this chapel is adorned with magnificent Gothic sgrafitti, and the entrance to it is flanked by two Celtiberian granite sculptures, attributed to the **Verraco** civilisation.

The museum was created in 1846 to house works taken from the suppressed monasteries and convents, though the most important pieces from them were taken to the Prado in Madrid, and to other art galleries. Nevertheless, the museum contains important prehistoric and Visigothic items found in sites around Segovia, including brooches, buckles and other ornaments. There is also a large collection of carvings and bas-reliefs, such as those taken from the altarpiece of the now lost Church of Santa Columba, an "Adoration of the Kings" by Berruguete and Spanish-Flemish panels, such as the 15th-century "Descent", known as the Contreras Panel, a tryptich by the Master of the Carnations and engravings by Dürer and Rembrandt.

*...ail of
the
...ce of
Santa
...umba
(16th
...tury).*

One of the rooms in the Zuloaga Museum.

DANIEL ZULOAGA MUSEUM (Plaza de Colmenares) The museum is housed in the Church of San Juan Bautista, popularly known as San Juan de los Caballeros, a 12th-century building constructed on the site of another church, to which belongs the nave, over which there is the now blunted tower, similar to that of the Church of San Esteban.

Two additional apses were built onto the church in the 13th century, giving it its final T-shaped structure, with a nave and two narrow aisles and three apses, of which only the central apse leads directly off from the nave. The south and west sides are surrounded by an atrium, and the most surprising element of the building is the cornice of the atrium and its portal, containing a typically Segovian adornment, a series of rosettes. The church was closed in the 19th century, and was bought in 1905 by the great ceramist Daniel Zuloaga,

who installed his kilns and workshops here, converting it into a studio which enjoyed international fame for many years. Ignacio Zuloaga, nephew of the founder, painted many of his best works in one of the apses. Daniel Zuloaga died in 1921, but his work was continued by his children, Juan, Esperanza and Teodora, who sold the building to the state after the Civil War. It has now been converted into a school and museum. The interior contains a picturesque assortment of furniture, antique artifacts, dazzling, metallic ceramic pieces and the oil and watercolour paintings of Ignacio and Daniel Zuloaga. A monument has been raised to Daniel Zuloaga in Segovia: a bust in Sepúlveda stone, by Emiliano Barral. It is a rugged work, full of character, with the windswept beard of Daniel splendidly achieved, giving the impression that the artist is watching us from the little garden at the head of the church.

View of the festivities for Saint Martha.

POPULAR FESTIVITIES

Segovia has been the scene for important festivities since time immemorial, some of them of great significance. For example, the great feast celebrated on the occasion of the coronation of Isabel the Catholic, the royal wedding of Philip II and Anne of Austria, and many more. The populace took an active part in these celebrations, and the Plaza Mayor was the scene for all of them, including the bullfights which took place in the city, until the bullring in the Campillo district was built in the 19th century. Easter is celebrated with solemn processions, the Good Friday procession being especially interesting for the beauty of the images carried, including the "Christ" by Gregorio Fernández, from the cathedral, that of the Gascones, "Soledad" from the Church of Santa Eulalia, the statues by Aniceto Marinas from the Church of San Millán, and many more.

Another splendid procession takes place for Corpus Cristi, commemorating the Miracle of the Sacred Host, which is carried out from the cathedral in a carriage. The origins of this festivity go back to 1410, and records show that it was formerly the event on which the city spent most money. The most outstanding elements of this procession are "La Tarasca", a diabolic she-devil, and the giants.

The fairs of San Juan and San Pedro, which take place in June, are the delight of young and old alike, attracting people from near and far. They include bullfights and popular dances, with a funfair in the Nueva Segovia district.

La Catorcena (The 14th) celebrates the miracle of Corpus Cristi, and is held on the first Sunday in September. It goes by this unusual name because originally the festivities were organised each year by a different one of the fourteen churches of the city.

The last Sunday in September is given over to the Virgen of La Fuencilsa, an emotive religious celebration which commences the week before with a morning mass attended by large numbers of worshippers to render homage to Our Lady.

A markedly traditional festivity is that of the patron saint of the city, Saint Frutos, which takes place on 25 October. This begins in the cathedral with the singing of the hymn to the "glorious Frutos". This day was traditionally dedicated to catching birds with lime, an excuse to enjoy a picnic in the country.

Besides these important fiestas, each district also celebrates its own, including those of San Marcos and la Cruz on 25 April and 3 May respectively, of El Carmen on 16 July and that of San Roque, in the San Millán district, on 16 August.

GASTRONOMY: RESTAURANTS AND *MESONES*

To speak of the cuisine of Segovia is to speak of roast lamb or suckling pig. The secret of the fame of these dishes lies in the excellent quality of the meat itself, from pastured animals, and in the way it is cooked in wood ovens, and seasoned with natural herbs, salt and water. Also exquiste is the trout from the Eresma, which delighted the Prince of Wales during his romantic journey around Spain in the last century. Neither should we forget the vegetables and pulses from the market gardens of San Marcos and San Lorenzo, or the typical *judiones* (beans) from San Ildefonso. Then there is the local pork and the various types of sausage (*chorizo, lomo de la olla, morcilla, chicharrones, picadillo*, etc) which

all make excellent apperitives. For dessert, there is nothing better than the *ponche*, a delicate biscuit made from eggs and marzipan, and the excellent local *yemas*, some of the tastiest to be found anywhere. The recipe for these is of long-standing tradition, passed down by the nuns. Until recently, the *Yemas* made by the Dominicans were famous along with the biscuits from San Antonio el Real and Santa Isabel and the almond pie made by the nuns of Peralta. Now, unfortunately these original delicacies are difficult to find.

Regarding restaurants, the full list would take up too much space. From El Azoguejo to Plaza Mayor, the streets are lined with fine places to eat, ranging from top restaurants, such as Cándido, Bernardino, Duque, etc, to the typical *mesones* around the Plaza Mayor, popular eating-houses serving the tastiest dishes.

Pottery and weaving are two of the outstanding crafts of Segovia.

MARKETS, SHOPS AND SHOPPING CENTRES

The best day to see Segovia at its most typical is on a Thursday market day when the city is filled with bustling life from the very early morning. Stands are set up all around Plaza de los Huertos, selling everything, from the choicest vegetables from the market gardens of the surrounding districts to pottery, clothes, records, and so on. The traditional Thursday market has been held since 1448, when Henry IV, then still a prince, exempted two markets from taxes, one formerly held in Plaza San Miguel and the other in the Mercado (Market) district.

The Thursday market is central to the activities of Segovia, and forms a colourful spectacle full of historical reminiscences. Crop and cattle farmers meet in the Azoguejo, next to the central building of the *Caja de Ahorros* to close deals with a handshake, as they have since medieval times.

Besides this popular market, there are other areas of the city to satisfy the needs of shoppers. The most fashionable shops are in Calle Fernández Ladreda, Calle Real and Calle José Zorrilla, the main thoroughfares of Segovia. The windows of the jewellers' shops display an impressive array of articles in gold and pearl, essential elements of Segovian traditional costume. In Calle Real, close to the former prison, a modern shopping centre has recently been built, where the latest fashions are on sale. The centre is also a pleasant spot for a stroll, as well as being interesting for its design, connecting Calle Real with Paseo del Salón.

LEISURE AND CULTURAL ACTIVITIES

Cultural life in Segovia centres to a large degree around the activities organised by the local Caja de Ahorros (saving bank) which take place at the Lozoya house. Throughout the year, exhibitions are held by Segovian artists or groups of artisans, such as the fair for arts and crafts at Easter.

The cultural life of the city has also been enriched by the opening of many private galleries and exhibition rooms, such as the well-known ''Casa del Siglo XV'', next to the statue of Juan Bravo, the Galería Machado, in Calle Daoíz, and Ladreda 25, in Calle Fernández Ladreda. Exhibitions of work by the students also take place at the School of Applied Arts and Crafts and the School of Engraving.

Despite the crises which have brought about the closure of such long-standing theatres as Cervantes and Sirenas, cinema-lovers will still find the latest films programmed in Segovia. Theatrical performances are somewhat less common, except for the fairs of San Juan and San Pedro, though the restoration of the Teatro Juan Bravo appears to herald a resurgence of the theatrical traditions of the city. During the fairs, a production is staged of the zarzuela ''La del Soto del Parral''. This is set in Segovia and features both professional singers in the main parts and local amateur performers in the secondary parts and chorus. International music and theatre festivals take place in Segovia during the first week of July, the performances held in various churches. The second week of July features a week of chamber music. There are seven performances some of which are held the cathedral and make use of the Baroque organs. Other take place in the square of the Alcázar or in the Palace of La Granja. Other events are organised by the City Council in conjunction with local amateur groups including popular dance festivals, featuring ''jotas'' and the ''paloteo''.

Building housing the Caja de Ahorros savings bank.

The Palace of San Ildefonso is surrounded by large, beautiful gardens.

ENVIRONS OF SEGOVIA

LA GRANJA DE SAN ILDEFONSO

La Granja is 11 kilometres from the city and 77 from Madrid, the town standing on the northern slopes of the Sierra de Guadarrama, at an altitude of 1,191 metres. The site, which enjoys a very pleasant climate, was known as long ago as the reign of Henry III, who used it for hunting. The buildings were extended by Henry IV, and were later donated by the Catholic Monarchs to the monks of El Parral. Philip II converted the original hunting lodge into a palace after the Alcázar in Madrid, El Pardo and El Escorial, and this building survived until it was damaged by fire during the reign of Charles II.

When Philip V and Isabel of Farnesio visited the site, they decided to use it as an occasional residence, and therefore purchased it from the monks of El Parral and commissioned the architect Teodoro Ardemans to construct the new palace. Work on this began on 1 April 1721 under the direction of Juan Román. The results were a large, rectangular monumental building with two parallel wings forming two inner courtyards, the Patio de Coches and the Patio de la Herradura, whilst the centre is occupied by the Patio de la Fuente, formerly a cloister and constructed in an austere style. The palace has two polished rubble walls, with architraved openings and slate-roofed turrets. The main front, looking over the gardens, was designed in 1734 by Juvara, and completed by Sachetti.

The interior of the palace contains two floors, the rooms of which are decorated with painted ceilings, for the most part the work of Bartolomé Rusca. There are some fine paintings by Lucas Jordán, Bassano, Houasse and Teniers, a splendid collection of sculptures in marble from Carrara, donated by Christina of Sweden, objects in glass, Oriental urns, fine wooden furniture and gilded bronze sculptures. The palace is surrounded by magnificent, extensive gardens, lakes and a huge park. The gardens and the statues contained in them are by a French team led by Boutelou and Carlier. Philip V brought Dutch lime trees, horse chestnuts and other trees to populate the great wood, and Renato Fremin and Juan Thierry were responsible for the statues and sculptures for the fountains, begun in 1721.

The full glory of the fountains can only be appreciated on certain feast days, particularly on Saint Louis' day, 25 August, as patron saint of San Ildefonso. This display is considered to be one of the finest in Europe.

Gardens of the Farm of San Ildefonso: Fountain of the Frogs.

The Great Waterfall features steps of multicoloured marble. ▷

Main front of the Palace of Riofrío.

Palace of Riofrío: room in Charles V's hunting pavilion and another room containing 150 paintings from the series ''The Life of Our Lord Jesus Christ''.

PALACE OF RIOFRIO

The Palace of Riofrío is ten kilometres from Segovia and twelve from San Ildefonso, and lies in a leafy oak wood. It was built in the 18th century at the behest of Isabel of Farnesio, widow of Philip V.

This is a Neo-Classical palace, of square groundplan and consisting of three unequal storeys with four almost identical façades. The building was designed by the Italian architect Virgilio Robaglio and the sculptures outside are by Pedro Sexmini. This is one of the Spanish monuments which most reminds us of Roman palaces, and the pinkish tone of its stone give the building unique charm.

The interior features an outstanding central courtyard and a fine main staircase, and the building also houses many valuable works of art, including paintings, tapestries and antique furniture.

The palace now also contains an important Hunting Museum.

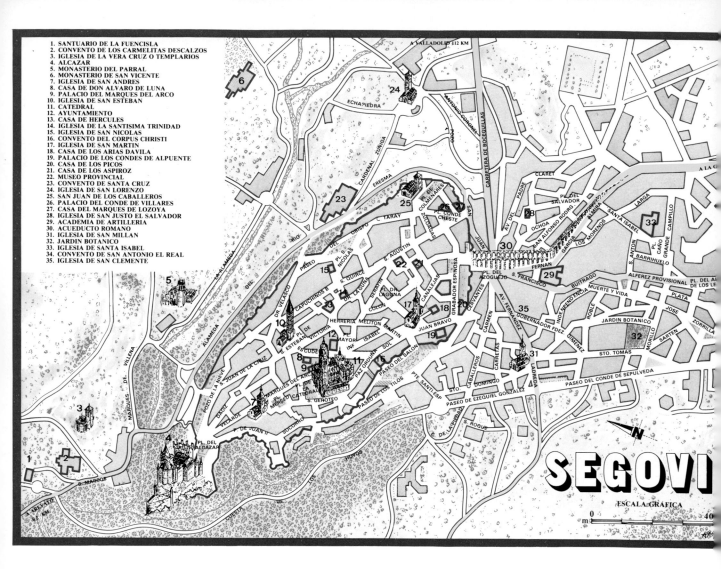

Contents

ESCUDO DE ORO, S.A. COLLECTIONS

Text, photographs, lay-out, design and printing by
EDITORIAL ESCUDO DE ORO, S.A.
Rights of total or partial reproduction and translation reserved.
Copyright of this edition for photographs and text:
© EDITORIAL ESCUDO DE ORO, S.A.
8th Edition - I.S.B.N. 84-378-1561-4
e-mail:editorial@eoro.com
http://www.eoro.com
Dep. Legal. B. 1524-2001

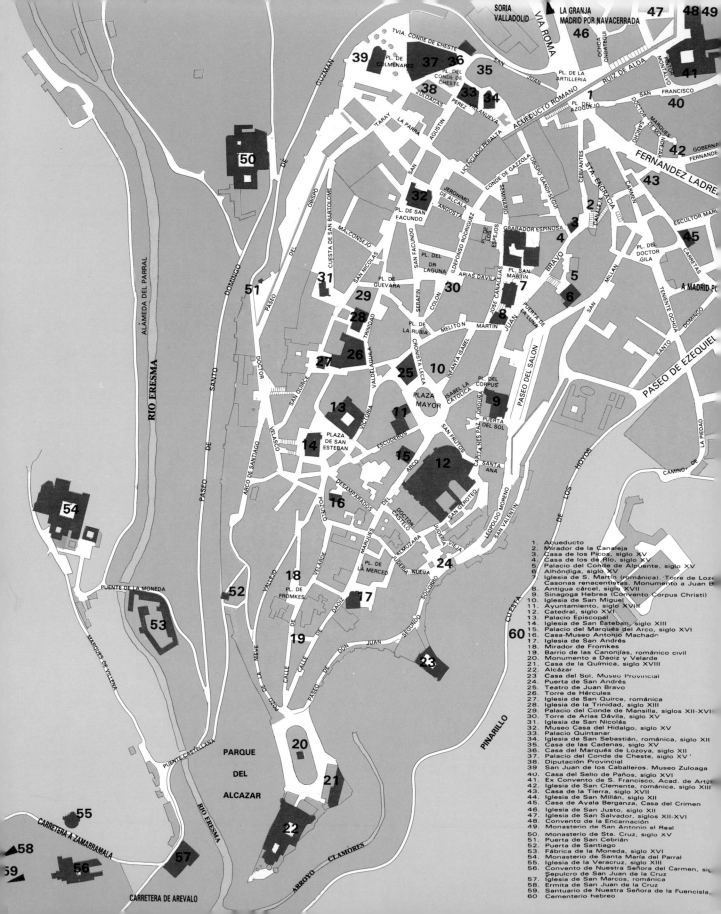

SORIA
VALLADOLID

LA GRANJA
MADRID POR NAVACERRADA

VIA ROMA

47 48 49

46

TVIA. CONDE DE CHESTE

PL. DE LA ARTILLERIA

PL. DE LA

RUIZ DE ALDA

39 PL. DE COLMENARES 37 36 35

38 33 34

PEREZ VILLANUEVA

ACUEDUCTO ROMANO

1

SAN FRANCISCO

40

42 GOBERNA FERNANDE

43

50

32 PL. DE SAN FACUNDO

GRABADOR ESPINOSA

2 ESCULTOR MARI

3

4

45 A MADRID P

31 30 29 28 27 26 25 10 9 13 14 11 15 16 17 18 19 20 21 22 23 24

PL. DE GUEVARA

PLAZA MAYOR

PLAZA DE SAN ESTEBAN

5 6 7 8 12

51 52 53 54 55 56 57 58 59 60

PARQUE DEL ALCAZAR

1. Acueducto
2. Mirador de la Canaleja
3. Casa de los Picos, siglo XV
4. Casa de los del Río, siglo XV
5. Palacio del Conde de Alpuente, siglo XV
6. Alhóndiga, siglo XV
7. Iglesia de S. Martín (románica). Torre de Loze
    Casonas renacentistas. Monumento a Juan B
8. Antigua cárcel, siglo XVII
9. Sinagoga Hebrea (Convento Corpus Christi)
10. Iglesia de San Miguel
11. Ayuntamiento, siglo XVIII
12. Catedral, siglo XVI
13. Palacio Episcopal
14. Iglesia de San Esteban, siglo XIII
15. Palacio del Marqués del Arco, siglo XVI
16. Casa-Museo Antonio Machado
17. Iglesia de San Andrés
18. Mirador de Fromkes
19. Barrio de las Canonjías, románico civil
20. Monumento a Daoiz y Velarde
21. Casa de la Química, siglo XVIII
22. Alcázar
23. Casa del Sol, Museo Provincial
24. Puerta de San Andrés
25. Teatro de Juan Bravo
26. Torre de Hércules
27. Iglesia de San Quirce, románica
28. Iglesia de la Trinidad, siglo XIII
29. Palacio del Conde de Mansilla, siglos XII-XVI
30. Torre de Arias Dávila, siglo XV
31. Iglesia de San Nicolás
32. Museo Casa del Hidalgo, siglo XV
33. Palacio Quintanar
34. Iglesia de San Sebastián, románica, siglo XII
35. Casa de las Cadenas, siglo XV
36. Casa del Marqués de Lozoya, siglo XII
37. Palacio del Conde de Cheste, siglo XV´
38. Diputación Provincial
39. San Juan de los Caballeros. Museo Zuloaga
40. Casa del Sello de Paños, siglo XVI
41. Ex Convento de S. Francisco, Acad. de Artil
42. Iglesia de San Clemente, románica, siglo XIII
43. Casa de la Tierra, siglo XVII
44. Iglesia de San Millán, siglo XII
45. Casa de Ayala Berganza, Casa del Crimen
46. Iglesia de San Justo, siglo XII
47. Iglesia de San Salvador, siglos XII-XVI
48. Convento de la Encarnación
49. Monasterio de San Antonio el Real
50. Monasterio de Sta. Cruz, siglo XV
51. Puerta de San Cebrián
52. Puerta de Santiago
53. Fábrica de la Moneda, siglo XVI
54. Monasterio de Santa María del Parral
55. Iglesia de la Veracruz, siglo XIII
56. Convento de Nuestra Señora del Carmen, sig
    Sepulcro de San Juan de la Cruz
57. Iglesia de San Marcos, románica
58. Ermita de San Juan de la Cruz
59. Santuario de Nuestra Señora de la Fuencisla,
60. Cementerio hebreo